THE BEST OF
INDIAN
COOKING

THE BEST OF INDIAN COOKING

Published in the United Kingdom by
CENTURION BOOKS LIMITED
52 George Street, London W1H 5RF

British Library Cataloguing in Publication Data

Mitchell, John
   Best of Indian Cooking
   I. Title
   ISBN: 0-948500-10-7

Photo credits:
Original photographs for the cover and inside pages, excluding
pages 1, 4 and 7/8 were taken by **Benno Gross & Associates**
at the Taj Mahal Hotel in Bombay and the Taj Palace Inter-Continental
in New Delhi. The photographs on pages 1, 4 and 7/8 were
provided by **Michael Freeman.**

Design and Artwork supplied by Centurion Design Forum Ltd. London.
Typesetting by Senator Graphics, London.
Printed in Hong Kong

THE BEST OF
INDIAN
COOKING

A Selection of Recipes from the Taj Group of Hotels

Edited by John Mitchell

CENTURION

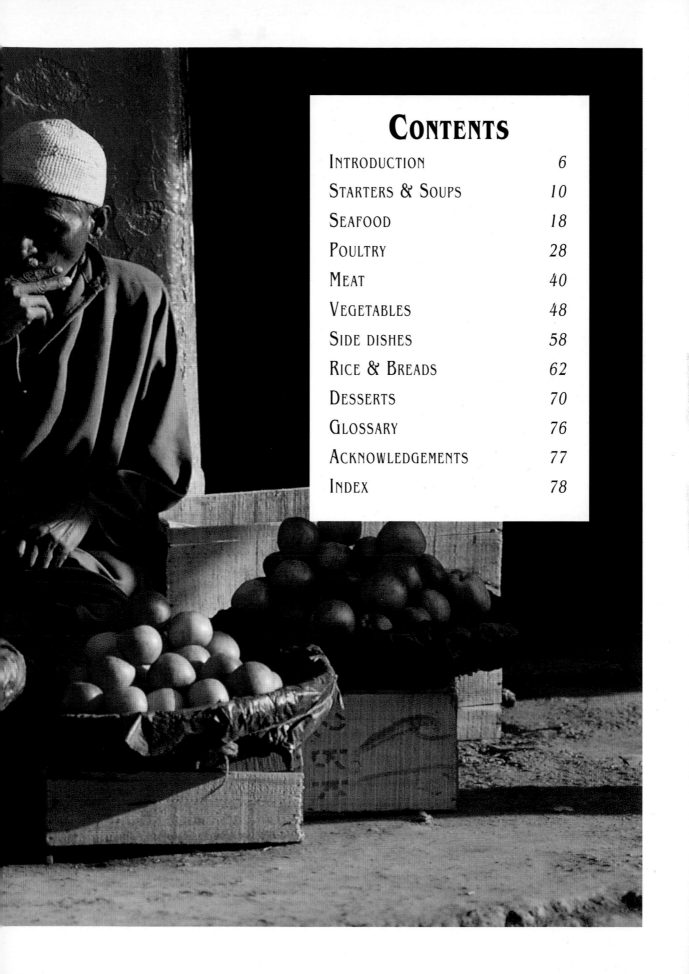

CONTENTS

Introduction

It's not that many years ago that an average westerner being asked to name four Indian dishes would have most likely replied (after some thought), chicken curry, beef curry, lamb curry, and . . . . (more hesitation) . . . . curried prawns. Tikka, Korma and Chapati would have been words familiar to but a few, and to most only the quantity of curry powder (pre-packed, naturally, and only available from the speciality shop in the high street) would have added variety to those basic ingredients.

But all has now changed. The explosion of emmigration from East to West over the past two or three decades has resulted in a proliferation of Asian markets and restaurants, throughout suburbs and country towns, which previously might only have been found in the larger cosmopolitan centres. In itself this has resulted in a wide acceptance of "foreign" foods yet perhaps an even greater influence has been the boom in packaged holidays which have made a journey from Bognor to Bombay, Dallas to Delhi and Madrid to Madras as commonplace today as a trip to the nearest seaside resort used to be.

While it's questionable how much ethnic history and culture is absorbed on such mass-market, time-sensitive peregrinations from museum to monument to ancient ruin, surely only the most hidebound ingestor can fail to become immutably influenced by the visits to local eateries. And should the journey be taken through India, then surely only the most insensitive palate can fail to discover new culinary delights to be enjoyed again and again long after all other experiences are only occasionally recalled by reference to photographs and scrapbooks.

In a book of this size it is impossible to comprehensively detail the vast cornucopia of all those delights India has to offer but even so, through the efforts of the two leading chefs from the Taj Group of Hotels the following pages offer a representative cross-section of the various regional dishes from the fiery curries of the South to the more subtle flavours of the North. Chef Satish Arora, chef culinaire and director of food production at the group's flagship, the Taj Mahal Hotel in Bombay, has provided recipes from the South and East while Chef Arvind Saraswat has done likewise from the Northern regions.

To make the recipes practical (and in most case relatively simple) for use in the domestic kitchen I have in editing made some changes from the original but only with the approval of the chefs. Also, as with other books in the series I have followed some standard guideline for quantities, measurement and servings, which are outlined below.

*The recipes have been written in metric measurements and the Imperial alternatives (bracketed) have been rounded up or down to serve as a practical, rather than a precise guide. Measurements over 75 grams (75 g) and 75 millilitres (75 ml) are shown in units of '25', and below that in 5 g/ml teaspoons (tsp) or 15 g/ml tablespoons (Tbsp).

*Varying combinations of spices go towards the preparation of a great Indian meal and enthusiastic cooks will, by trial and error, change an original recipe to suit personal tastes. The fact that the same basic ingredients, treated with individual imagination, can produce such differing results is what, to many, makes cooking a pleasure rather than a chore.

*When preparing any spicy food it should be appreciated that while a number of ingredients may add 'sharpness' and 'bite', it is the chilli that provides the 'fire'. Though some chillies are comparatively mild all should be used sparingly when preparing a meal for a number of people. Rather than inflict suffering on one delicate palate far better to serve side-dishes of chilli sauce or freshly chopped chillies to cater for those with hardier digestive systems.

*A home-cooked Indian meal will generally consist of a number of dishes (fish, meat and vegetables) served simultaneously with rice or bread (most likely both), chutneys and condiments. With that in mind the quantities shown in most of the following recipes are intended for serving 4-6 people.

*Ingredients are generally written using their most commonplace English name with an occasional reference to the glossary. The English names of the recipes are not necessarily a direct translation of the original but are written to be practical. For simplicity, the index and picture captions use only the English names.

Spice Pastes

SPICE PASTES

A variety of pastes are called for in many of the recipes which follow and while some can be purchased ready-made it may prove convenient to prepare your own in advance. The quantities given here are only intended as a guide; you should prepare more or less depending on likely requirements.

GINGER PASTE

Chop 200 g (9 oz) of ginger, place in a blender with 4 tablespoons of water and process to a fine paste.

CHILLI PASTE

Remove the stems from 150 g (5 oz) of dried red chillies and shake out the seed. Soak in tepid water for 30 minutes, then drain and place in a blender with 3 tablespoons of water. Process until smooth.

GARLIC PASTE

Soak 100 g (4 oz) of garlic cloves in water for 20 minutes, then peel and place in a blender with 100 ml (4 fl oz) water. Process until smooth.

CASHEWNUT PASTE

Shell 200g (7 oz) of unsalted cashewnuts and blend together with 150 ml (5 fl oz) water to produce a smooth paste.

BROWN ONION PASTE

Slice 1 kilo (2¼ lbs) of onions and fry in oil over a moderate heat until golden, then remove and spread on kitchen paper to cool. Place in a blender together with 100 g (4 oz) of natural yoghurt and process until smooth.

BOILED ONION PASTE

Roughly chop 1 kilo (2¼ lbs) of onions and place in a saucepan with 3 bay leaves, 3 black cardamoms and approximately 150 ml (5 fl oz) water. Boil until the onions are cooked and the liquid has almost evaporated, then transfer to a blender and process until smooth. Do not store.

NOTE:

To store the cashewnut, chilli, garlic and ginger pastes, cover with oil and place in the refrigerator for up to 3 days.

To store the brown onion paste place in a sterilised, airtight container and keep in the refrigerator for up to 10 days.

abs and Salad

CHEMEEN OOLARTHIATHU
(deep-fried spicy prawns)

700 g (1¹/₂ lbs) small prawns
1 tsp turmeric
1 tsp salt
2 Tbsp fresh lemon juice
2 onions
3 tomatoes
6 cloves garlic
oil for deep-frying
8 curry leaves
1 tsp ground coriander
1 tsp ground black pepper
freshly chopped coriander

Batter
2 Tbsp cornflour
1 Tbsp superfine flour
2 eggs
1.5 Tbsp red chilli paste

Shell and de-vein the prawns, sprinkle with turmeric, salt and lemon juice and set aside for 30 minutes. Chop the onions, tomatoes and garlic. Heat the oil in a large shallow pan until moderately hot. Coat the prawns with prepared batter and deep-fry until golden and crispy, then remove with a slotted spoon and drain on absorbent paper. Then, heat a small quantity of oil in a fresh pan and add the curry leaves. When they start to crackle, add the onion and garlic and sauté until brown. Next, add the tomato, ground coriander and pepper and continue to stir until the tomato is cooked, then add the prawns and toss to coat evenly. Continue to cook until the sauce has been almost completely absorbed, then adjust seasonings to taste. To serve: transfer to a large dish and garnish with freshly chopped coriander.

To make the batter: sift the cornflour and flour into a bowl, break in the eggs and add the chilli powder. Pour in just sufficient cold water to produce a thick batter and mix thoroughly.

KORI KEMPU BEZULE
(chilli chicken)

8 chicken breast fillets
1 tsp turmeric powder
0.5 tsp salt
1 Tbsp garlic paste
3 green chillies
oil for deep frying
10 curry leaves
4 Tbsp natural yoghurt

Batter
4 Tbsp cornflour
2 Tbsp superfine flour
salt
2 eggs
1.5 Tbsp red chilli paste
1 Tbsp freshly chopped coriander

Remove the skin and cut chicken breasts into 15 mm wide strips. Place in a shallow dish, sprinkle with turmeric powder and salt and cover with garlic paste, then set aside for 30 minutes. Chop the chillies. Heat the oil in a pan until moderately hot. Coat the chicken in the prepared batter and place in the hot oil. Fry until golden and crispy. Then remove with a slotted spoon. Next, heat a fresh pan, add the curry leaves, chillies, yoghurt and chicken and toss until the yoghurt has evaporated. Adjust seasonings to taste and transfer to a serving dish.

To make the batter: sift the cornflour, flour and a little salt into a mixing bowl. Break in the eggs, add the chilli, coriander and just sufficient cold water to produce a thick batter. Mix well.

KADUKU ERAL
(mustard prawns)

600 g (1¼ lbs) prawns
1 large onion
2 tomatoes
4 cloves garlic
2 Tbsp oil
1 Tbsp mustard seeds
8 curry leaves
1 heaped Tbsp chilli powder
salt to taste
chopped coriander leaves

Shell and de-vein the prawns, then wash under running water, pat dry and set aside. Chop finely the onion, tomatoes and garlic. Heat the oil in a pan until very hot, then add the mustard seeds and curry leaves. When they start to crackle, immediately add the onion and garlic and sauté until softened. Next add the tomato and cook for 4-5 minutes, then add the chilli powder and stir well. Lower the heat and add the prawns. Cook for 10-12 minutes, stirring frequently, then season with salt to taste. To serve: transfer to a large plate and garnish with chopped coriander leaves.

Mustard prawns

SAMOSA
(deep-fried pasties)

750 g (1¾ lbs) potatoes
150 g (5 oz) green peas
25 mm (1 inch) knob fresh ginger
3 green chillies
ghee for frying
0.5 tsp cumin seeds
1 tsp red chilli powder
1 tsp ground cumin
1 tsp pomegranate seeds
salt to taste
1 tsp garam masala
1 heaped Tbsp freshly chopped coriander
1 Tbsp fresh lemon juice

Dough:
250 g (9 oz) plain flour
pinch of salt
2 Tbsp ghee
pinch of ajwain

Boil the potatoes and allow to cool, then peel and cut into 5 mm (¼ inch) cubes. Boil the peas until tender, then drain in a colander. Chop the ginger and chillies. Heat 1 tablespoon of ghee in a pan, add the cumin seeds and stir over a moderate heat until they start to crackle, then add the ginger and green chilli and stir for a further 15 seconds. Add the potato, peas, chilli powder, ground cumin, pomegranate seeds and salt and sauté for 2-3 minutes, then transfer to a mixing bowl. Add the garam masala, freshly chopped coriander and lemon juice and mix well. Allow to cool, then divide into 20 equal portions. Divide the dough into 10 balls and place on a lightly oiled surface, then flatten with a rolling pin into rounds, approximately 60 mm (2½ inches). Cut each round in half, dampen the edges and shape into cones. Stuff a portion of mixture into each cone and seal by pressing firmly. Coat the samosas with flour. Heat more ghee in a large pan and deep-fry the samosas for 12-15 minutes until cooked, golden and crispy.

To make the dough: sift the flour and salt into a mixing bowl. Melt the ghee and add to the bowl together with 100 ml (4 fl oz) of warm water. Add the ajwain and knead well, if necessary adding a little extra warm water to ensure the dough does not crumble. Cover the bowl and set aside for 30 minutes.

ALOO TIKKI
(potato cakes)

1 kilo (2¼ lbs) potatoes
2 Tbsp gram flour
1 tsp salt
1 onion
20 mm (1 inch) knob fresh ginger
2 green chillies
200 g (7 oz) green peas
75 g (3 oz) ghee
2 tsp cumin seeds
1 tsp red chilli powder
1 tsp ground coriander
1 tsp chaat masala
1 tsp garam masala
1 Tbsp freshly chopped coriander
100 g saunth
100 g (4 oz) mint chutney

Boil the potatoes, allow to cool, then mash. Dry roast the flour, allow to cool, then add to the potato, together with the salt. Mix thoroughly. Chop finely the onion, ginger and chillies. Cook the peas in boiling water and drain in a sieve. Heat half the ghee in a pan, add the cumin seeds and when they start to crackle add the onion and sauté until golden. Next, add the peas, ginger, chilli, chilli powder, ground coriander, and chaat masala. Stir well, then add the potato, garam masala and freshly chopped coriander. Stir again to mix thoroughly, then remove from the pan and allow to cool. Divide the mixture into 12 equal portions, roll into balls, then flatten and shape into round patties. Finally, heat the remaining ghee on a griddle, or in a heavy-based non-stick frying pan and fry the patties, turning once, until both sides have a dark-golden crust. To serve: crumble into individual serving dishes, add saunth and mint chutney and garnish with raw onion rings.

Samosas and Potato Cakes

KHARWANI JHINGA
(prawn soup)

500 g (1¼ lbs) small prawns
2 small raw mangoes
1 large onion
6 green chillies
1 Tbsp freshly chopped coriander
1 tsp oil
0.5 tsp ground turmeric
pinch of asafoetida
1 Tbsp gram flour
550 ml (1 pint) thin coconut milk
275 ml (½ pint) thick
coconut milk
salt to taste

Shell and de-vein the prawns. Peel the mangoes and cut into small dice. Chop the onion and chillies and crush coarsely with half the coriander. Heat the oil in a saucepan, add the crushed onion mixture and stir. Then add the turmeric and asafoetida and sauté for 3 minutes. Add the prawns together with 75 ml (3 fl oz) of water and stir for 1-2 minutes, then add the mango and cook over a moderate heat for 10-12 minutes. Next, mix the flour with the thin coconut milk and add to the prawns. Bring to the boil, then lower heat and allow to simmer, stirring frequently, until the soup starts to thicken. Then, reduce heat and stir in the thick coconut milk. Bring back to boiling point, then immediately remove pan from the heat and add the remaining coriander. Finally, add salt to taste, stir well and transfer to a soup tureen. Serve immediately.

DAHI KA SHORBA
(spicy yoghurt soup)

800 g (1¾ lbs) natural yoghurt
1 small onion
1 small tomato
4 Tbsp butter
1 tsp cumin seeds
1 tsp chopped ginger
1 tsp chopped green chilli
0.5 tsp ground turmeric
1 Tbsp freshly chopped coriander
100 ml (4 fl oz) cream
salt to taste

Whisk the yoghurt. Chop the onion and tomato. Melt the butter in a saucepan, add the cumin seeds and stir until they start to crackle. Then, add the onion, tomato, ginger, chilli and turmeric and stir for 1 minute. Remove the pan from the heat and allow to cool slightly, then return to the heat and add the yoghurt, coriander and half the cream. Bring to the boil, then stir in the remaining cream and season with salt to taste. Transfer to individual soup cups and serve immediately.

TAMATAR KA SHORBA
(spiced tomato soup)

1.5 kilos (3 ¼ lbs) ripe tomatoes
25 mm (1 inch) knob fresh ginger
3 cloves garlic
6 fresh red chillies
1 Tbsp roasted coriander seeds
0.5 tsp ground turmeric
8 curry leaves
salt to taste
2 Tbsp oil
1 tsp cumin seeds
1 tsp mustard seeds
garlic croutons

Cut the tomatoes in half. Chop the ginger, garlic and chillies. Place the tomatoes in a saucepan, add the ginger, coriander, turmeric and 4 curry leaves and cover with water – approximately 1.5 litres (2½ pints). Bring to the boil, then lower heat and allow to simmer for 30 minutes. Strain through a sieve into a fresh saucepan and return to the heat. Add salt to taste and simmer for a further 12-15 minutes. In the meantime, heat the oil in a pan, add the cumin seeds, mustard seeds, garlic, chilli and remaining curry leaves and stir until the seeds start to crackle, then add to the soup and stir well. Transfer to a soup tureen and garnish with garlic croutons.

KASHMIRI SHORBA
(meat ball soup)

175 g (6 oz) fresh mutton
1 tsp chopped ginger
1 tsp freshly chopped coriander
0.5 tsp chopped green chilli
1 egg white
1 tsp fresh lemon juice
salt to taste
freshly ground black pepper

Stock:
2 Tbsp butter
1 tsp chopped garlic
1 tsp chopped ginger
0.5 tsp red chilli powder
100 g (4 oz) natural yoghurt
1 Tbsp freshly chopped coriander
1.25 litres (2¼ pints) meat stock
2 Tbsp fresh lemon juice
few drops orange colouring

Mince the mutton and mix with the ginger, coriander, chilli, egg white, lemon juice, salt and pepper. Divide the mixture into 24 equal portions and shape into marble-size balls. Add the meat balls to simmering stock and cook for 10 minutes. To serve; place the meat balls in individual soup bowls and add the stock.

To make the stock: melt the butter in a large saucepan, add the garlic and ginger and sauté over a moderate heat for 30 seconds. Remove the pan from the heat and add the chilli powder, yoghurt and coriander. Stir well and return the pan to the heat, then pour in the stock and bring to the boil. Next, add the lemon juice and colouring, lower the heat and allow to simmer for 8-10 minutes, then adjust seasonings to taste.

SAMUDRI KHAZANA TAK-A-TIN
(seafood platter)

250 g (9 oz) small fresh prawns
500 g (1¼ lbs) non-fatty fish fillets
2 dried red chillies
2 onions
125 g (4 oz) boiled potatoes
3 fresh green chillies
100 g (4 oz) ghee
1 tsp ajwain
1 Tbsp ginger paste
2 tsp garlic paste
100 g (4 oz) seafood mince
300 g (10 oz) tomato purée
3 Tbsp fresh lemon juice
1 tsp garam masala
0.5 tsp chaat masala
1 Tbsp freshly chopped coriander
salt to taste

Shell and de-vein the prawns and cut the fish into 25 mm (1 inch) chunks. Soak the dried chillies in warm water for 20 minutes, then chop finely. Chop the onion, potatoes and green chillies. Heat the ghee on a griddle, add the prawns and fish and stir over a moderate heat for 2 minutes, then remove and set aside. Add the ajwain to the pan and stir for 3 seconds, then add the ginger and garlic pastes, the onion and green chillies. Reduce the heat and sauté for 2-3 minutes, then add the red chillies, seafood mince and tomato purée. Stir well and cook until the sauce is reduced by half, then add the prawns, fish and potato and stir well. Next, holding two metal spatulas vertically, chop the seafood and potato, stirring and folding frequently. Continue until the mixture is fully cooked. Finally, increase the heat, add the lemon juice, garam masala, chaat masala, coriander and salt and stir for a further 30 seconds. Serve immediately with an Indian bread.

KAKEDA KARI
(crab curry)

8 small crabs
4 onions
100 ml (4 fl oz) oil
1 Tbsp black peppercorns
1 Tbsp coriander seeds
12 dried red chillies
0.5 tsp black cumin seeds
4 cardamom seeds
8 cloves
50 mm (2 inch) cinnamon stick
3 Tbsp tamarind pulp
2 Tbsp grated coconut
0.5 tsp ground turmeric
75 ml (3 fl oz) thick coconut milk
salt to taste
freshly chopped coriander leaves

Chop the crabs into bite size pieces. Slice 2 of the onions and chop the others. Heat 2 tablespoons of oil in a pan and fry the sliced onion until brown, then remove and drain on kitchen paper. Lightly roast the peppercorns, coriander seeds, chillies, cumin, cardamom, cloves and cinnamon then grind these with the tamarind and fried onion to produce a fine masala paste. Heat a further 2 tablespoons of oil in a fresh pan and stir-fry the coconut and turmeric for 2-3 minutes, then grind to a fine paste. Next, heat the remaining oil and sauté the chopped onion. Add the crabs and cook for 6 minutes, stirring frequently, then add the masala and coconut pastes. Stir well, add 75 ml (3 fl oz) water and bring to the boil, then lower heat and allow to simmer for 5 minutes. Add the coconut milk and bring back to the boil, then lower heat, adjust seasonings to taste and cook over a moderate heat until the sauce starts to thicken. Transfer to a large serving dish and garnish with freshly chopped coriander.

HARA KAKEDA
(spicy crabs)

8 small crabs
4 Tbsp vinegar
8 spring onions
4 green chillies
3 cloves garlic
15 mm (³/₄ inch) knob fresh ginger
1 Tbsp finely chopped dill
2 Tbsp freshly chopped coriander
1 tsp red chilli powder
1 tsp ground roasted cumin seeds
1 tsp crushed peppercorns
salt to taste
75 g (3 oz) mayonnaise

Place the crabs in a large pan of boiling water, add the vinegar and cook until the crabs turn a bright red, approximately 30 minutes. Allow to cool, then carefully remove all the meat and place in a mixing bowl. Wash the crab shells and dry thoroughly. Chop the spring onions, chillies, garlic and ginger and add to the crabmeat together with all the remaining ingredients. Blend well, then stuff the mixture into the crab shells and place in the refrigerator for 1 hour before serving.

CHINGRI MALAI
(prawn coconut curry)

800g (1³/₄ lbs) fresh prawns
1 tsp ground turmeric
salt to taste
150 ml (5 fl oz) mustard oil
2 Tbsp ginger paste
2 Tbsp garlic paste
100 g onion paste
1 Tbsp green chilli paste
350 ml (12 fl oz) thick coconut milk

Shell and de-vein the prawns, then wash under cold running water and pat dry. Rub turmeric and salt into the prawns and set aside for 10 minutes. Heat the oil in a pan and sauté the prawns over a moderate heat for 2-3 minutes, then remove with a slotted spoon and set aside. Re-heat the oil, add the ginger and garlic pastes and stir over a moderate heat for 2 minutes, then add the onion and chilli pastes and continue to stir for a further 2 minutes. Next, add the coconut milk and bring to the boil, then lower heat and allow to simmer for 5-6 minutes. Finally, add the prawns and continue to cook until the sauce has reduced by two-thirds. Adjust seasonings to taste and serve with steamed rice.

Sauce for Baked Lobster *(following page)*

2 kilos (4¹/₂ lbs) tomatoes
200 g (7 oz) soft butter
1 tsp red chilli powder
125 ml (4 fl oz) fresh cream
salt to taste

To make the sauce: quarter the tomatoes and place in a pan over a moderate heat. Allow to simmer until the tomato is reduced by half, then strain through a fine sieve into a fresh pan. Place over a low heat, add the butter and chilli powder and cook for 8 minutes, stirring frequently. Finally, add the fresh cream and salt to taste and stir until boiling then remove from the heat.

LOBSTER KIKA
(baked lobster)

4 medium-size lobsters
4 Tbsp vinegar
2 onions
6 spring onions
6 green chillies
25 mm (1 inch) knob fresh ginger
3 cloves garlic
1 kilo (2¼ lbs) spinach
100 g (4 oz) butter
1 tsp cumin seeds
1 Tbsp red chilli paste
2 Tbsp freshly chopped coriander
salt to taste
100 ml (4 fl oz) fresh cream
pinch of nutmeg
freshly ground black pepper
100 g (4 oz) grated cheddar cheese

Clean the lobsters. Bring a large pan of water to the boil, add the vinegar and cook the lobsters until they turn bright red, approximately 30 minutes. Then split the lobsters in half lengthways, carefully remove all the meat from the body, claws and tail and cut into bite-size chunks. Wash the shells and place in a warming oven. Chop the onions, spring onions, chillies, ginger and garlic. Wash the spinach thoroughly under cold running water. Heat two thirds of the butter in a pan and add the cumin seeds. When they start to crackle add the onion, ginger, garlic and chilli paste and cook for a further 6 minutes, stirring continuously. Next, add the lobster, coriander, salt to taste and half the cream. Stir well and bring to boiling point, then remove pan from the heat. Meanwhile, boil the spinach, plunge in cold water to refresh, then chop. Heat the remaining butter in a fresh pan and sauté the spring onion for 3-4 minutes, then add the spinach, nutmeg and pepper and cook for a further ten minutes, stirring frequently. Next, add the remaining cream, stir well and bring almost to boiling point, then remove pan from heat. Take the reserved shells from the oven, arrange a layer of spinach in each and fill with the lobster. Pour the prepared sauce over the lobsters, top with grated cheese and place in a hot oven. Bake until the cheese has melted and the tops are golden brown. Serve immediately.

GOAN LOBSTER KORI
(curried lobster)

4 lobsters
2 Tbsp dried tamarind
2 tomatoes
2 onions
6 green chillies
25 mm (1 inch) knob fresh ginger
150 g (5 oz) fresh coconut
10 dried red chillies
1 Tbsp cumin seeds
1 Tbsp coriander seeds
10 black peppercorns
1 tsp ground turmeric
3 Tbsp oil
salt to taste

Cut the lobsters into pieces. Soak the tamarind in cold water for 30 minutes, then squeeze and reserve the pulp. Slice the tomatoes, onions, green chillies and ginger. Grind together the coconut, red chillies, cumin, coriander, peppercorns and turmeric. Mix with 100 ml (4 fl oz) of water to form a smooth paste. Heat the oil in a pan, add the tomato, onion, chilli and ginger and sauté for 5 minutes, then add the coconut paste and cook over a moderate heat for a further 10 minutes. Add the lobster, season with salt to taste and allow to simmer for 2-3 minutes, then add the tamarind pulp and cook until the lobster is done.

Baked Lobster and Curried Lobster

MADRAS MEEN KARI
(Madras mackerel curry)

800 g (1 3/4 lbs) mackerel fillets
2 onions
3 tomatoes
4 cloves garlic
6 green chillies
3 Tbsp oil
1 Tbsp mustard seeds
0.5 tsp fenugreek seeds
1 tsp ground turmeric
1 Tbsp red chilli powder
1 Tbsp ground coriander
1 tsp ground cumin
10 curry leaves
2 Tbsp grated coconut
2 tsp tamarind pulp
salt to taste

Cut the mackerel into bite-size cubes. Chop the onions, tomatoes, garlic and chillies. Heat the oil in a pan, add the mustard and fenugreek seeds and, when they start to crackle, add the onion and sauté until brown. Add the garlic and continue to sauté for a further 6 minutes, then add the turmeric, chilli powder, coriander, cumin and curry leaves. Stir for 5 minutes, then add the coconut and continue to stir for a further 5 minutes. Next, add the tomato and tamarind and allow to cook slowly for 4-5 minutes, then add the mackerel and a small quantity of water. Retain over a moderate heat until the mackerel is cooked, then add the chopped chilli and salt to taste. Stir well and transfer to a large dish. Serve with steamed rice.

MEEN KOLAMBU
(South Indian fish curry)

650 g (1 1/2 lbs) white fish fillets
2 onions
1 tomato
1 Tbsp red chilli powder
1.5 tsp ground coriander
3 Tbsp tamarind water
3 Tbsp oil
1 tsp cumin seeds
0.5 tsp fenugreek seeds
1 Tbsp aniseed
1.5 Tbsp ginger paste
1.5 Tbsp garlic paste
0.5 tsp ground turmeric
8 curry leaves
salt to taste

Cut the fish into 12 serving-size pieces. Slice the onions and chop the tomato. Mix the chilli and coriander with the tamarind water. Heat the oil in a pan, add the cumin, fenugreek and aniseed and when they start to crackle add the onion slices. Cook over a low heat until the moisture has evaporated but do not let the onion brown. Next, add the ginger and garlic pastes and sauté for 5 minutes, then add the turmeric and curry leaves and stir well. Add the tomato and cook until soft, then add the tamarind water and allow to simmer for 10 minutes. Finally, add the fish and retain over a moderate heat until cooked, then adjust seasonings to taste and transfer to a large dish. Serve with plain steamed rice.

TULSI ANARDANA MAACHI
(spicy sole fillets)

800 g (1¾ lbs) sole fillets
8 cloves garlic
1 Tbsp ground turmeric
salt to taste
75 ml (3 fl oz) fresh lemon juice
3 Tbsp flour
75 ml (3 fl oz) olive oil
3 tomatoes
8 spring onions
25 mm (1 inch) knob fresh ginger
1 Tbsp finely chopped sweet basil
1 tsp ground pomegranate seeds
1 Tbsp chaat masala
1 tsp black salt
1 tsp ground cumin
1 tsp freshly chopped coriander

Cut the fish into serving-size pieces and place in a shallow dish. Crush the garlic and mix with the turmeric, salt and lemon juice. Pour the mixture over the fish and set aside for 30 minutes. Then, remove the fish from the marinade and dust with flour. Heat the oil in a pan and fry the fish until golden and crispy, then remove with a slotted spoon and arrange on a serving dish. Allow to cool. Meanwhile, chop the tomatoes, spring onions and ginger and mix with all the remaining ingredients, except the coriander. Then, spread the mixture over the fish and place in the refrigerator for 90 minutes. Just prior to serving sprinkle the chopped coriander over the fish.

MACHCHLI AMRITSARI
(fried fish steaks)

800 g (1¾ lbs) whole firm fish
4 Tbsp gram flour
4 Tbsp plain flour
4 Tbsp cornflour
pinch of salt
1 Tbsp ajwain
2 tsp red chilli powder
2 Tbsp ginger paste
2 Tbsp garlic paste
2 eggs
2 Tbsp fresh lemon juice
2 tsp chaat masala
lemon wedges
onion relish

Clean and prepare the fish and cut into 20 mm (1 inch) thick steaks. Sift the three flours and the salt into a mixing bowl and add the ajwain chilli powder, ginger paste, garlic paste, eggs and lemon juice. Pour in approximately 100 ml (4 fl oz) of cold water and mix well to produce a fairly thin batter. Place the fish steaks in the batter and set aside for 1 hour. Heat the oil in a large frying pan. Remove the fish from the batter with a slotted spoon and place in the hot oil. Fry until the steaks are cooked and crispy on both sides, then transfer to a large plate and sprinkle with chaat masala. Garnish with lemon wedges and serve with an onion relish.

NADRU MACHCHLI
(fish curry with lotus stem)

800 g (1³/₄ lbs) pomfret fillets
200 g (7 oz) canned lotus roots
6 tomatoes
200 ml (7 oz) mustard oil
1 tsp asafoetida granules
1 tsp cloves
1 tsp sugar
1 heaped Tbsp red chilli paste
2 tsp powdered ginger
1 heaped Tbsp ground fennel
salt to taste
1 Tbsp chopped coriander

Cut the fish into serving-size pieces. Cut the lotus roots into diamond-shape pieces and chop the tomatoes. Heat the oil to smoking point, then remove from heat and allow to cool (this is to remove the smell of the mustard oil). Re-heat the oil and add the pieces of fish. Fry over a moderate heat until the fish is golden brown, then remove and set aside. Add the lotus root to the pan and fry until half cooked, then remove and set aside. Next, fry the asafoetida granules in the same oil, then remove and crush into a powder. Re-heat the oil and add the sugar and cloves. Once the sugar starts to caramelise, add the chilli paste for 5 seconds, then immediately add 2 tablespoons of cold water. Now, add the tomato and cook until the oil starts to separate, then add the ginger, fennel and salt to taste. Add the lotus root and fry for 5 minutes, then pour in 500 ml (18 fl oz) of cold water and bring to the boil. Lower the heat, add the fish and the asafoetida and allow to simmer for 10-12 minutes. Finally, adjust seasonings, add the coriander and stir. Transfer to a large dish and serve with boiled or steamed rice.

Fish Curry with Lotus Stem

MEEN POLLICHATHU
(fish in banana leaves)

8 mackerel
4 shallots
6 cloves garlic
30 mm (1¼ inch) knob fresh ginger
6 green chillies
10 curry leaves
10 whole cloves
10 cardamom seeds
15 black peppercorns
50 mm (2 inch) cinnamon stick
¼ nutmeg
1 tsp ground turmeric
1 Tbsp red chilli powder
2 Tbsp vinegar
2 Tbsp coconut oil
salt to taste
banana leaves

Clean and prepare the fish. Chop the shallots, garlic, ginger and chillies and place in a blender together with the curry leaves. Blend to produce a smooth paste. Next, grind together the cloves, cardamons, peppercorns, cinnamon and nutmeg, then add this to the mixture in the blender. Add the turmeric, chilli powder, vinegar, coconut oil and salt and blend again. Coat the fish evenly with the spice-paste and set aside for 30 minutes. Cut the banana leaves into squares suitable for wrapping around the fish. Heat the pieces of banana leaf over an open fire and place a fish in the centre of each. Wrap and secure, then place over a charcoal fire or under a hot grill until the fish is cooked, approximately 15 minutes. Open the leaves and transfer to individual plates. Serve with rice or Indian breads.

Fish in Banana Leaves

TANDOORI MURG
(barbecued chicken)

2 chickens, about 800 g
(1¾ lbs) each
2 Tbsp fresh lemon juice
1 tsp salt
butter for basting

Marinade
200 g (7 oz) natural yoghurt
2 Tbsp garlic paste
2 Tbsp ginger paste
1 Tbsp red chilli powder
1 tsp garam masala
1 tsp ground cumin
salt to taste
2 Tbsp groundnut oil
2 Tbsp fresh lemon juice
few drops orange colouring

Remove the skin from the chickens and make deep incisions, 3 on each breast, 3 on each thigh and 2 on each drumstick. Sprinkle the lemon juice over the chickens and rub in the salt, then set aside for 15 minutes. Place the chickens in the prepared marinade and leave in the refrigerator for 5 hours, turning occasionally. Next remove the chickens from the marinade and arrange in a roasting tin with the breasts facing downwards or, alternatively, if the oven has a rotisserie, thread on a skewer. In either case ensure the chickens are not touching each other. Cook in a hot oven for 12-15 minutes, basting frequently with the butter. To serve: cut the chicken into pieces and garnish with onion rings, lemon and tomato wedges.

To make the marinade: whisk the yoghurt in a bowl, add the remaining ingredients and mix thoroughly.

Note: Traditionally the chicken would be cooked in a tandoor, a clay oven heated by charcoal, but the above method, suitable for a western domestic kitchen, will give very satisfactory results, although the flavour will not be quite the same.

TELANGANA MURG
(fried chicken)

2 chickens
2 onions
10 fresh red chillies
3 Tbsp poppy seeds
4 Tbsp grated coconut
1 Tbsp coriander seeds
1 Tbsp cumin seeds
1 Tbsp black peppercorns
3 Tbsp oil
1 Tbsp garlic paste
1 Tbsp ginger paste
10 curry leaves
1 tsp ground turmeric
1 Tbsp fresh lemon juice
salt to taste
freshly chopped coriander

Cut the chickens into pieces. Chop the onions and chillies. Dry roast the poppy seed and coconut and pound to a paste. Dry roast the chilli, coriander seeds, cumin and peppercorns and grind to a powder. Heat the oil in a pan and sauté the onion until brown, then add the garlic and ginger pastes and continue to stir for 5 minutes. Next, add the curry leaves, turmeric and poppy seed paste and sauté for a further 5 minutes. Add the pieces of chicken and the ground masala and cook for 5-6 minutes, stirring frequently, then add a little water and cook over a moderate heat until the chicken is tender. Finally, stir in the lemon juice, add salt to taste and transfer to a serving dish. Garnish with freshly chopped coriander.

MURG KI MOKAL
(chicken julienne in a spicy sauce)

800 g (1³/₄ lbs) boned chicken
breasts
150 g (5 oz) onions
250 g (9 oz) natural yoghurt
150 g (5 oz) ghee
1 tsp cumin seeds
2 Tbsp ginger paste
2 Tbsp garlic paste
1 tsp red chilli powder
0.5 tsp ground turmeric
salt to taste
2 Tbsp cashew nut paste
2 tsp garam masala
0.5 tsp ground mace
1 tsp ground cardamom
2 Tbsp toasted almond flakes

Remove skin from the chicken and cut the meat into 10 mm
(¹/₂ inch) thick strips. Blanch in boiling water for 2 minutes, then
drain. Slice the onions and whisk the yoghurt. Heat the ghee in a
pan and sauté the onion over a moderate heat until golden, then
add the cumin and stir. Dissolve the ginger and garlic pastes in
4 tablespoons of water, add to the pan and stir for 1 minute, then
remove from the heat and stir in the yoghurt. Next, return the pan
to the heat and cook until the fat rises, then add the pieces of
chicken and stir for a further minute. Add 150 ml (5 fl oz) of water
and bring to the boil, then lower heat and allow to simmer until
the chicken is tender. Add the chilli powder, turmeric and salt, stir
well, and remove pan from heat. Dissolve the cashew nut paste in
a little water and add to the pan, then return to the heat and bring
back to the boil. Finally, add the garam masala, mace and
cardamom, stir well and adjust seasonings to taste. Transfer to a
large dish, garnish with toasted almond flakes and serve with an
Indian bread.

MURG NU FARCHA
(double-fried chicken)

2 chickens, approx. 1 kilo
(2¹/₄ lbs) each
2 onions
3 tomatoes
oil for deep-frying
8 cloves
8 green cardamom seeds
2 Tbsp garlic paste
1 Tbsp ginger paste
1 tsp ground turmeric
1.5 Tbsp red chilli paste
1 tsp roasted ground cumin
1 tsp ground coriander
6 eggs
1 Tbsp freshly chopped coriander
salt to taste
75 g (3 oz) flour

Cut the chicken into bite-size pieces. Chop the onions and
tomatoes. Heat 3 tablespoons of oil, add the onion together with
the cloves and cardamoms and sauté until brown, then add the
garlic and ginger paste and continue to sauté for 6 minutes. Add
the turmeric and 1 tablespoon of the chilli paste and continue to
stir for 5-6 minutes. Next, add the tomato and cook over a
moderate heat until the tomato is soft, then add the chicken,
cumin and coriander and cook for a further 8-10 minutes, stirring
frequently. Add a small quantity of cold water to the pan and allow
to simmer until the chicken is cooked, then remove the chicken
and drain on kitchen paper. Meanwhile, break the eggs into a
bowl, add the coriander, salt and remaining chilli paste and beat
lightly. Finally, dust the chicken pieces with flour, coat with the
beaten egg and deep-fry in more oil until golden and crispy. Serve
immediately with a barbecue sauce.

MURG MAKHAN MASALA
(barbecued chicken in tomato gravy)

2 barbecued chickens
800 g (1¾ lbs) tomatoes
250 g (9 oz) onion
30 mm (1¼ inch) knob fresh ginger
3 green chillies
small bunch fresh coriander
200 g (7 oz) butter
1 tsp red chilli powder
1 tsp ground fenugreek
salt to taste
200 ml (7 fl oz) single cream

Cut each chicken into 8 pieces. Chop the tomatoes, onions, ginger, chillies and coriander. Melt half the butter in a pan, add the onion and sauté until golden brown, then add the ginger and half the chopped green chilli. Stir for 1 minute, then add the chopped tomato, red chilli powder and salt and continue stirring until the fat comes to the surface. Next, add the chicken and cook for 2-3 minutes, then add the remaining butter, fenugreek and half the coriander. Allow to simmer for 2 minutes until the butter has melted, then adjust seasonings to taste and add the cream. Bring to the boil, add the remaining chopped chilli and coriander and stir well. Serve with Pulao Rice.

Barbecued Chicken in Gravy

MURG CAFREAL
(spicy roast chicken)

2 chickens
1 tsp salt
6 cloves garlic
30 mm (1¼ inch) knob fresh ginger
8 green chillies
4 sprigs fresh coriander
3 sprigs fresh mint
6 cloves
8 cardamom seeds
1 Tbsp cumin seeds
10 black peppercorns
50 mm (2 inch) cinnamon stick
2 Tbsp vinegar
3 Tbsp oil
fried onion slices

Cut the chickens in half and make slits in the skin on the breasts, thighs and drumsticks. Sprinkle salt over the chicken. Chop the garlic, ginger, chillies, coriander and mint and blend together with the cloves, cardamoms, cumin, peppercorns, cinnamon and vinegar to produce a smooth paste. Rub the paste over the chicken and set aside in the refrigerator for 1½ hours. To cook: heat the oil in a large roasting pan and sear the chicken until golden, then add a small quantity of cold water and cook over a low heat for 45-50 minutes, or until the chicken is tender. Transfer to a serving dish and garnish with fried onion slices. Serve with garlic rice.

Spicy Roast Chicken

Chicken Balls in Gravy (recipe next page)

34

Shahi Murg Galouti
(chicken balls in gravy)

700 g (1½ lbs) boned
chicken breasts
20 mm (1 inch) knob fresh ginger
2 green chillies
2 stalks fresh coriander
2 Tbsp cashew nut paste
2 tsp garam masala
salt to taste
2 Tbsp cornflour
oil for deep-frying
100 ml (4 fl oz) cream
2 Tbsp chopped coriander
large pinch mace
large pinch nutmeg
large pinch ground cardamom

Gravy:
150 g (5 oz) onions
20 mm (1 inch) knob fresh ginger
2 green chillies
3 Tbsp ghee
1 heaped tsp turmeric
300 ml (10 fl oz) chicken stock

Mince the chicken meat. Chop the ginger, chillies and coriander and place in a mixing bowl together with the chicken, cashew nut paste, half the garam masala and salt to taste. Mix well and divide the mixture into balls, approximately 25 mm in diameter, then dust with the cornflour. Heat the oil in a pan until very hot and deep-fry the chicken balls until golden brown, then remove with a slotted spoon and drain on absorbent paper. Add the chicken balls to the boiling gravy and stir gently, then add the cream, ground coriander and remaining garam masala and cook until the gravy reaches coating consistency. Finally, add the mace, nutmeg and cardamom, adjust seasonings to taste and stir well. Transfer to a large plate and serve with an Indian bread.

To make the gravy: chop the onions, ginger and chillies. Heat the ghee in a pan, add the chopped vegetables and stir-fry over a moderate heat for 2-3 minutes, then add the turmeric, salt and stock and bring to the boil. Continue boiling for 5 minutes, or until the stock is reduced by half.

Kori Gassi
(chicken curry)

2 chickens
2 large onions
8 cloves garlic
8 dried red chillies
4 Tbsp oil
1 Tbsp cumin seeds
0.5 tsp fenugreek seeds
0.5 tsp black peppercorns
1 tsp ground turmeric
175 g (6 oz) grated coconut
125 ml (4 fl oz) thick coconut milk
salt to taste

Halve the chickens. Chop the onions and garlic. Heat a small quantity of oil and fry the garlic, chillies, cumin, fenugreek, peppercorns and turmeric, then mix with the grated coconut and grind to produce a smooth paste. Add 3 tablespoons of water to the paste and bring to the boil, then lower heat and allow to simmer for 30 minutes, stirring frequently. Heat the remaining oil in a fresh pan and sauté the onion until golden brown, then add the chicken and continue to cook for 6 minutes, turning once or twice. Add the masala paste and simmer for a further 30 minutes. Finally, add the coconut milk and salt to taste and cook until the sauce is thick. Serve with an Indian bread or a rice pancake.

MURG DHANIWAL KORMA
(chicken with dry ginger and coriander)

2 chickens, about 850 g (2 lbs) each
150 g (5 oz) onions
400 g (14 oz) natural yoghurt
5 green cardamoms
1 tsp ground cinnamon
100 g (4 oz) melted ghee
300 ml (10 oz) chicken stock
0.5 tsp ground turmeric
1 tsp ground coriander
salt to taste
3 Tbsp brown onion paste
1 tsp ground ginger
2 tsp freshly chopped coriander

Remove skin from the chickens and cut each bird into 8 pieces. Chop the onions. Whisk the yoghurt with 100 ml (4 fl oz) of water and slowly bring to the boil, stirring continuously, then add the cardamom, cinnamon and ghee and continue to stir for 1 minute. Add the stock, turmeric, ground coriander and salt and bring to the boil, then add the chicken and onion. Lower the heat and allow to simmer, stirring occasionally, until the chicken is cooked, then add the onion paste, ginger and freshly chopped coriander and stir to mix thoroughly. Transfer to a large dish and serve with plain steamed rice.

MURG XACUTTI
(chicken with coconut)

2 chickens
2 onions
3 Tbsp oil
1 Tbsp grated ginger
1 tsp grated garlic
150 g (5 oz) grated coconut
15 dried red chillies
1 Tbsp poppy seeds
1 tsp ground turmeric
1 Tbsp coriander seeds
1 Tbsp black peppercorns
1 Tbsp aniseed
0.5 tsp fenugreek seeds
0.5 tsp grated nutmeg
8 cardamom seeds
30 mm (1¼ inch) cinnamon stick
3 Tbsp tamarind pulp
salt to taste

Cut the chickens into serving-size pieces. Chop the onions. Heat a very small quantity of oil in a heavy-based pan and roast separately the ginger, garlic, coconut, chillies, poppy seeds, turmeric, coriander, peppercorns, aniseed, fenugreek, nutmeg, cardamoms and cinnamon, then grind these ingredients to produce a coarse masala paste. Wash out the paste remaining in the grinder with a little cold water and reserve. Heat the remaining oil in a fresh pan and sauté the onion until brown, then add the masala paste and cook until the oil rises. Next, add the chicken pieces and cook over a fairly high heat, stirring frequently, until the chicken is half cooked. Add the reserved liquid and bring to the boil, then add the tamarind, stir well, and continue to cook over a low heat until the chicken is tender. Add salt to taste and transfer to a serving dish.

Roast Duck and Spicy Duck

THARAV ERACHY
(roast duck)

2 young ducks
4 boiled potatoes
1 large onion
1 tsp chopped garlic
1 Tbsp chopped ginger
10 dried red chillies
1 Tbsp coriander seeds
1 Tbsp cumin seeds
1 Tbsp aniseed
1 tsp black peppercorns
1 tsp ground turmeric
8 cardamom seeds
50 mm (2 inch) cinnamon stick
2 Tbsp vinegar
salt to taste
3 Tbsp coconut oil
3 Tbsp ghee
500 ml (18 fl oz) thick coconut milk

Cut the duck into serving-size pieces. Quarter the potatoes and slice the onion. In a heavy-based pan dry-roast the garlic, ginger, chillies, coriander, cumin, aniseed, peppercorns, turmeric, cardamom and cinnamon, then grind together and rub into the duck. Sprinkle the vinegar over the duck, season with salt and set aside for one hour. Heat the oil and ghee in a pan and sauté the duck until tender, then remove the duck and drain on kitchen paper. Next, add the potatoes to the pan and fry until golden, then remove to a strainer. Pour off all but one tablespoon of oil and in this fry the onion for 3-4 minutes. Then, replace the duck and pour in the coconut milk. Bring to the boil, then lower heat and allow to simmer until the sauce starts to thicken. Finally, adjust seasonings to taste and stir well, then transfer to a serving dish and arrange the potatoes around the duck.

DUM KI BATHAK
(spicy duck)

2 young ducks
4 green chillies
20 mm (1 inch) knob fresh ginger
250 g (9 oz) natural yoghurt
3 Tbsp cashew nut paste
3 Tbsp almond paste
3 Tbsp ghee
1 tsp cumin seeds
4 cardamoms
4 cloves
3 Tbsp onion paste
1 Tbsp garlic paste
10 mint leaves
pinch of saffron
2 tsp warm milk
2 Tbsp fresh lemon juice
1 tsp white pepper
salt to taste

Cut the ducks into 8 pieces each. Chop the chillies and ginger. Whisk the yoghurt and mix with the cashew nut and almond pastes. Heat the ghee in a pan, add the cumin, cardamoms and cloves and when they start to crackle add the onion paste. Sauté for 3-4 minutes, then add the chillies, ginger and garlic paste and continue to sauté for a further 6 minutes. Add the pieces of duck and brown evenly, then add the yoghurt and mint leaves. Bring to the boil, then lower heat and allow to simmer for 15 minutes. Mix the saffron with the warm milk and add to the pan. Cover with a tightly fitting lid and, if necessary, seal with dough to ensure no steam escapes. Continue to cook for approximately 20 minutes, then remove the lid and add the lemon juice, pepper and salt to taste. Stir well before transferring to a serving dish.

KOLA URUNDAI KOLAMBU
(minced lamb patties)

1 kilo (2¼ lbs) fresh lamb
15 mm (¾ inch) knob fresh ginger
5 cloves garlic
6 fresh green chillies
6 spring onions
6 roasted curry leaves
1.5 Tbsp aniseed
3 Tbsp chopped cashew nuts
3 Tbsp roasted lentils
2 eggs
salt to taste

Sauce:
3 Tbsp chopped cashew nuts
3 Tbsp coconut flesh
3 large tomatoes
4 green chillies
75 ml (3 fl oz) oil
6 green cardamoms
1 Tsp cumin seeds
100 ml (4 fl oz) fresh cream

Mince the lamb and put three-quarters in a pan. Cover with water and boil until cooked, then remove. Drain and mix with the remaining uncooked meat. Chop the ginger, garlic, chillies and spring onion and add to the meat, together with the curry leaves, aniseed, cashew nuts and lentils. Grind to a smooth texture then break in the eggs and add salt to taste. Mix well and divide into small balls. Bring the prepared sauce to the boil and add the meat balls, then lower the heat and allow to simmer for 5-6 minutes until the sauce thickens. Serve immediately.

To make the sauce: grind the cashew nuts with a small quantity of cold water to produce a smooth paste and do likewise with the coconut. Chop the tomatoes and slice the chillies. Heat the oil until it starts to smoke, then add the cardomoms and cumin seeds. When they start to crackle add the cashew nut and coconut pastes and the chillies and lower the heat. Continue to cook for 10 minutes, stirring frequently, then add the tomatoes and sauté for a further 6 minutes. Finally, stir in the cream.

DUM KI RAAN
(roast leg of lamb)

2 knuckle end, legs of lamb
1 tsp salt
25 mm (1 inch) knob fresh ginger
6 cloves garlic
8 green chillies
1 Tbsp cumin seeds
1 tsp cardamom seeds
0.5 tsp black peppercorns
100 g (4 oz) cashew nuts
2 Tbsp freshly chopped coriander
350g (12 oz) natural yoghurt
2 Tbsp fresh lemon juice
large pinch of saffron
1 tsp red chilli powder
1 tsp ground coriander
125 ml (4 fl oz) oil
3 bay leaves
3 cinnamon sticks

Trim excess fat from the lamb and rub with salt. Chop the ginger, garlic and chillies and grind these together with the cumin, cardamom, cloves, peppercorns, cashew nuts and freshly chopped coriander. Whisk the yoghurt and add to the paste together with the lemon juice, saffron, chilli powder and ground coriander. Add the lamb and turn to coat evenly, then set aside for 1 hour. To cook: heat the oil in a roasting pan and sear the lamb (with marination) on both ideas. Add the bay leaves and cinnamon sticks and cover the pan. Cook in a slow oven, basting occasionally with the pan juices (and, if necessary, sprinkle a little warm water on the meat to keep it moist) until the meat is soft. Remove the cinnamon and bay leaves and transfer to a serving dish. Garnish with spring onions, tomato and cucumber slices.

GOSHT GULBARGA
(lamb korma)

600 g (1¼ lbs) boned lamb
2 large onions
6 cloves
8 cardamom seeds
1 Tbsp cumin seeds
50 mm (2 inch) cinnamon stick
small piece of nutmeg
4 Tbsp oil
2 bay leaves
2 Tbsp ginger paste
2 Tbsp garlic paste
1 Tbsp red chilli powder
2 tsp ground turmeric
3 Tbsp coconut paste
3 Tbsp poppy seed paste
2 Tbsp roasted ground coriander
salt to taste
freshly chopped coriander

Cut the lamb into bite-size cubes. Chop the onions. In a heavy-based pan dry-roast the cloves, cardamoms, cumin seeds, cinnamon and nutmeg and crush into a masala. Heat the oil in a pan, add the bay leaf, onion and crushed masala and sauté until the onion is golden. Add the ginger and garlic pastes and continue to stir over a fairly high heat for a further 6 minutes. Then, add the chilli powder, turmeric and lamb. Pour in 100 ml (4 fl oz) of water and cook over a low heat for approximately one hour, until the lamb is almost cooked. Finally, add the coconut paste, poppy seed paste, ground coriander and salt and continue to simmer for a further 15-20 minutes until the meat is tender. Transfer to a serving dish and garnish with freshly chopped coriander.

ROGANJOSH
(mutton curry)

1 kilo (2¼ lbs) mutton
250 g (9 oz) natural yoghurt
150 g (5 oz) ghee
0.5 tsp cloves
0.5 tsp green cardamoms
3 Tbsp ginger paste
3 Tbsp garlic paste
1 tsp red chilli powder
1 heaped Tbsp ground coriander
salt to taste
100 g (4 oz) brown onion paste
1 tsp garam masala
0.5 tsp ground cardamom
1 Tbsp freshly chopped coriander
0.5 tsp ground mace

Cut the mutton into 20 mm (1 inch) chunks and place in a shallow dish. Whisk the yoghurt, pour over the meat and set aside for one hour. Heat the ghee in a pan, add the cloves and cardamoms and sauté over a moderate heat for 15 seconds. Add the ginger and garlic pastes, chilli powder, coriander and salt and stir for 30 seconds, then add the mutton and yoghurt. Bring to the boil, add 800 ml (1¼ pints) of water and bring back to the boil, then cover the pan and allow to simmer until the meat is almost cooked. Next, add the onion paste and stir over a moderate heat until the fat rises and the lamb is tender, then add the garam masala, ground caradamom, chopped coriander and mace. Stir, adjust seasonings to taste and transfer to a large dish. Serve with rice or an Indian bread.

BHEJA MASALA
(spicy brain)

700 g (1½lbs) mutton brain
200 g (7 oz) onions
250 g (9 oz) small tomatoes
30 mm (1¼ inch) knob fresh ginger
100 g (4 oz) ghee
2 tsp chopped green chillies
1 Tbsp ginger paste
1 Tbsp garlic paste
1 tsp red chilli powder
0.5 tsp ground turmeric
1 tsp ground coriander
salt to taste
0.5 tsp ground fenugreek
2 tsp garam masala
1.5 Tbsp freshly chopped coriander

Clean and prepare the brain carefully to ensure it doesn't crumble. Chop the onion and all but one of the tomatoes. Slice the ginger and chop three-quarters. Quarter the remaining tomato and cut the remaining ginger into julienne strips and set these aside for garnish. Heat the ghee in a frying pan and sauté the onion over a moderate heat until golden, then add the chopped ginger and green chilli and stir for 30 seconds. Dissolve the ginger paste, garlic paste, chilli powder, turmeric and ground coriander in 150ml (5 fl oz) of water and add to the pan. Stir for 1 minute, then add the chopped tomato and salt to taste, and continue to stir until the fat separates. Next, add the brain and stir gently for 2-3 minutes, then add the fenugreek, garam masala and freshly chopped coriander. Stir well, adjust seasonings to taste and transfer to a serving dish. Garnish with the reserved tomato and ginger.

Spicy Brain

44

PAYA
(spiced trotters)

16 lamb trotters
4 green cardamoms
2 black cardamoms
6 cloves
50 mm (2 inch) cinnamon stick
2 bay leaves
2 tsp red chilli powder
300 g (10 oz) ghee
2 tsp ginger paste
2 tsp garlic paste
0.5 tsp ground turmeric
1 Tbsp ground coriander
300 g (10 oz) natural yoghurt
salt to taste
3 Tbsp brown onion paste
1.5 Tbsp garam masala
1.5 Tbsp freshly chopped coriander

Clean the trotters, then blanch and drain. Pour 5 litres (8¾ pints) of water over the trotters and bring to the boil. Add half the cardamoms, cloves, cinnamon, bay leaves and chilli powder and lower the heat. Allow to simmer for 2 hours. Then, heat the ghee in a pan, add the remaining cardamoms, cloves, cinnamon and bay leaf and stir until it starts to crackle. Dissolve the ginger paste, garlic paste, turmeric, ground coriander and remaining chilli powder in 4 tablespoons of water and add to the pan. Stir for 2 minutes, then add the yoghurt and salt to taste and bring to boil. Add the onion paste and reduce heat to low. Stir until the fat rises, then add the trotters together with the stock and bring back to the boil. Cover the pan and allow to simmer for 15 minutes. Finally, add the garam masala and freshly chopped coriander and stir well. Remove the cinnamon sticks and adjust seasonings to taste before transferring to a large plate. Serve with naan.

PORK SORPOTEL
(pork and liver stew)

800 g (1¾ lb) fresh pork
200 g (7 oz) pork liver
20 mm (1 inch) cinnamon stick
1 tsp ground turmeric
10 cloves
15 black peppercorns
2 large onions
10 dried red chillies
4 Tbsp vinegar
4 Tbsp oil
2 tsp garlic paste
1.5 Tbsp ginger paste
salt to taste

Place the pork meat and liver in a saucepan, add the cinnamon, turmeric, cloves and peppercorns and cover with water. Bring to the boil and cook until the meat is tender, then remove and cut into small pieces. Strain and reserve the stock. Chop the onions. Chop the chillies and grind together with the vinegar to produce a smooth paste. Heat the oil in a pan, add the onion and sauté until brown, then add the garlic and ginger pastes. Continue to sauté for 5-6 minutes, then add the chilli paste, pork meat, liver, salt and 100 ml (4 fl oz) water. Bring to the boil, then lower heat and allow to simmer until the pork is very soft and the sauce has reduced by half.

Spiced Pork Chops and Pork Vindaloo

RISHAD GOAN
(spiced pork chops)

8 pork chops
4 fresh green chillies
6 cloves garlic
2 Tbsp red chilli paste
2 Tbsp ginger paste
1.5 tsp ground turmeric
1 Tbsp roasted ground cumin
1 Tbsp freshly ground black pepper
salt to taste
3 Tbsp vinegar
2 Tbsp oil
freshly chopped coriander leaves

Trim excess fat from the chops and arrange on a large platter. Chop the chillies and crush the garlic, then combine these with the chilli paste, ginger paste, turmeric, cumin, pepper, salt and vinegar. Mix well and spread over the chops. Set aside for 30 minutes. Next, arrange the chops on an oiled roasting tray and place in a pre-heated moderate oven until thoroughly cooked. Serve garnished with a little freshly chopped coriander.

PORK VINDALOO
(hot pork curry)

800 g (1¾ lbs) lean pork
4 Tbsp vinegar
2 tomatoes
2 large onions
30 mm (1¼ inch) knob fresh ginger
8 cloves garlic
4 red chillies
15 peppercorns
1 Tbsp cumin seeds
3 Tbsp oil
1.5 tsp ground turmeric
salt to taste

Cut the pork into bite-size cubes. Mix 1 tablespoon of vinegar with water and rinse the pork. Chop the tomatoes. Chop the onions, ginger, garlic and chillies and grind these together with the peppercorns, cumin and remaining vinegar to produce a smooth paste. Rub the paste over the pork and set aside for 30 minutes. Then, heat the oil in a pan and sauté the pork for 10 minutes. Add the tomato and turmeric and continue to stir until the tomato is soft. Next, pour in sufficient hot water to cover the pork and cook until the meat is tender. Add salt to taste and transfer to a serving dish.

DAHI ALOO
(potatos in yoghurt)

500 g (1¼ lbs) potatoes
150 g (5 oz) natural yoghurt
1 onion
6 fresh green chillies
25 mm (1 inch) knob fresh ginger
2 dried red chillies
1 tsp black peppercorns
3 Tbsp ghee
1 tsp cumin seeds
6 bird pepper chillies
6 curry leaves
1 Tbsp garlic paste
0.5 tsp ground turmeric
salt to taste
freshly chopped coriander

Peel the potatoes and cook in boiling salted water, then drain and cut into cubes. Whisk the yoghurt. Chop the onion, fresh green chillies and ginger. Crush the dried red chillies and peppercorns. Heat the ghee in a pan, add the cumin seeds, bird pepper chillies and curry leaves and when the seeds start to crackle add the onion, green chilli and ginger. Cook until the onion becomes transparent, then add the garlic paste and turmeric and sauté for 5-6 minutes. Add the potatoes together with the yoghurt and bring almost to the boil, then lower heat and allow to simmer for 2 minutes. Finally add the crushed red chilli, pepper and salt to taste and stir well. Transfer to a serving dish and garnish with a little freshly chopped coriander.

TIL MOONGFALI ALOO
(sesame potatoes)

500 g (1¼ lbs) small new potatoes
4 large green chillies
20 mm (1 inch) knob fresh ginger
3 Tbsp oil
1 tsp cumin seeds
1 Tbsp garlic paste
1 Tbsp white sesame seeds
2 Tbsp chopped peanuts
1 tsp roasted ground cumin
1 tsp red chilli powder
1.5 Tbsp grated coconut
1 tsp garam masala
salt to taste
freshly chopped coriander leaves

Par-boil the potatoes and set aside. Chop the chillies and ginger. Heat the oil in a pan and add the cumin seeds, chilli and ginger. When the seeds start to crackle add the garlic paste and sauté for 3 minutes, then add the potatoes and stir. Next, add the sesame seeds, chopped peanuts, ground cumin, chilli powder, coconut and garam masala and cook for 5 minutes, stirring frequently. Add salt to taste, stir well and transfer to a serving dish. Garnish with freshly chopped coriander.

KAJU KHUMB CURRY
(mushroom curry)

600 g (1¼ lbs) fresh mushrooms
150 g (5 oz) onions
250 g (9 oz) tomatoes
75 g (3 oz) ghee
1 tsp onion seeds
1 tsp cumin seeds
2 Tbsp ginger paste
2 Tbsp garlic paste
1 tsp red chilli powder
½ tsp turmeric
1 tsp ground coriander
150 g (5 oz) yoghurt
salt to taste
75 g (3 oz) cashew nuts
freshly chopped coriander

Blanch the mushrooms and drain in a colander. Chop the onions and tomatoes. Heat the ghee in a pan, add the onion and sauté over a moderate heat until brown, then add the onion seed and cumin. Stir until the cumin starts to crackle, then add the ginger paste, garlic paste, chilli powder, turmeric, ground coriander and 4 tablespoons of water. Stir for 30 seconds, then add the tomato and continue to stir until the oil separates. Remove the pan from the heat, add the yoghurt and season with salt to taste. Stir well, then return to the heat, add 400 ml (14 fl oz) of water and bring to the boil. Allow to simmer until the fat separates and the sauce is smooth, then add the mushrooms and continue to simmer for a further 5 minutes. Finally, add the cashew nuts and freshly chopped coriander, adjust seasonings to taste and stir well. Transfer to a large dish and serve with rice or an Indian bread.

Curried Mushrooms

SUBZI KOCHAR
(vegetable potpourri)

200 g (7 oz) cauliflower
200 g (7 oz) carrots
200 g (7 oz) potatoes
200 g (7 oz) pumpkin
1 green pepper
25 mm (1 inch) knob fresh ginger
oil for deep frying
125 g (4 oz) ghee
1 tsp cumin seeds
1 tsp rye
2 tsp red chilli powder
0.5 tsp ground turmeric
salt to taste
200 g (7 oz) green peas
1 tsp chopped garlic
2 tsp mango powder
1 Tbsp freshly chopped coriander

Break the cauliflower into florets and cut the carrots, potatoes, pumpkin and green pepper into thick strips. Cut the ginger into julienne strips. Heat the oil and deep-fry the cauliflower, carrot, potato and pumpkin for 3 minutes, then remove and drain off excess oil. Heat the ghee in a pan, add the cumin and rye and stir for 20 seconds, then add the chilli powder, turmeric and salt and mix well. Next, add the fried vegetables, green pepper and peas and stir for one minute, then pour in 200 ml (7 fl oz) of water. Bring to the boil, then lower heat and allow to simmer until the vegetables are almost cooked. Finally, add the ginger, garlic, mango powder and coriander and continue to cook until the vegetables are tender. Adjust seasonings to taste and transfer to a serving dish.

PANEER MUTTAR
(feta cheese and pea curry)

600 g (1¼ lbs) feta cheese
200 g (7 oz) green peas
2 onions
5 tomatoes
100 g (4 oz) ghee
5 green cardamoms
1 black cardamom
5 cloves
25 mm (1 inch) cinnamon stick
1 bay leaf
pinch of mace
1 Tbsp chopped ginger
2 tsp chopped green chillies
1 tsp red chilli powder
0.5 tsp ground turmeric
2 Tbsp ginger paste
2 Tbsp garlic paste
salt to taste
2 tsp garam masala
1 Tbsp freshly chopped coriander

Cut the cheese into bite-size cubes. Blanch the peas. Chop the onions and tomatoes. Heat the ghee in a pan. Add the cardamoms, cloves, cinnamon, bay leaf and mace and sauté over a moderate heat until the seeds start to crackle, then add the onion, ginger and chopped chillies. Continue to stir until the onion is golden, then add the chilli powder and turmeric and stir for 30 seconds. Next, dissolve the ginger and garlic pastes in 2 tablespoons of water and add to the pan. Stir for 30 seconds, then add the tomato and salt to taste and continue stirring until the fat rises. Add 400 ml (14 fl oz) of water and bring to the boil. Add the cottage cheese and peas, stir, and cook for 4-5 minutes, then remove cinnamon stick. Finally, add the garam masala and coriander, stir and adjust seasonings to taste.

Vegetable Potpourri and Feta Cheese & Peas Curry

DAL HARYALI
(lentils with spinach)

300 g (10 oz) lentils
0.5 tsp ground turmeric
1 tsp red chilli powder
0.5 tsp salt
150 g (5 oz) spinach
4 onions
20 mm (1 inch) knob fresh ginger
6 cloves garlic
2 fresh green chillies
3 Tbsp ghee
2 tsp garam masala
100 g (4 oz) butter
2 Tbsp freshly chopped
coriander leaves

Wash the lentils and place in a saucepan with sufficient water to cover. Add the turmeric, chilli powder and salt and simmer over a moderate heat until almost cooked. Remove any scum from the surface, then drain and set aside. Cut the spinach into thick strips and blanch. Chop the onions, ginger, garlic and chillies. Heat the ghee in a pan, add the onion, ginger, garlic and chilli and sauté over a moderate heat until the onion is golden, then add the lentils together with 400 ml (14 fl oz) of water. Stir well and bring to the boil, then add the spinach, garam masala and butter and allow to simmer for 5 minutes. Finally, sprinkle in the chopped coriander and adjust seasonings to taste. Stir and transfer to a serving dish.

PORCHERI
(vegetable stew)

150 g (5 oz) lentils
200 g (7 oz) green bananas
100 g (4 oz) yam
1 tsp ground turmeric
1 Tbsp red chilli powder
1 tsp salt
1 Tbsp cumin seeds
100 g (4 oz) grated coconut
1 Tbsp palm sugar
1.5 Tbsp coconut oil
1 Tbsp mustard seeds
6 curry leaves

Wash the lentils and cook with sufficient water until tender, then drain and set aside. Cut the bananas and yam into small pieces and place in a saucepan. Cover with water and bring to the boil, then add the turmeric, chilli powder and salt. Cook over a moderate heat until tender, then grind the cumin with half the grated coconut and add to the pan. Add the palm sugar and lentils, stir well and bring back to the boil, then remove from the heat. In the meantime, heat the oil and add the mustard seeds. When they start to crackle add the curry leaves and remaining coconut. Cook for 1 minute, then add to the vegetables and stir to blend thoroughly. Transfer to a large dish and serve immediately.

MIRCHI KA SALAN
(green chillies in gravy)

350 g (12 oz) fresh long green chillies
oil for frying
2 shallots
1.5 Tbsp sesame seeds
3 Tbsp chopped fresh peanuts
1.5 Tbsp coriander seeds
3 Tbsp dessicated coconut
1.5 Tbsp cumin seeds
1 tsp onion seeds
6 curry leaves
1 tsp mustard seeds
0.5 tsp fenugreek seeds
1 Tbsp ginger paste
2 Tbsp garlic paste
1 tsp ground turmeric
1 tsp red chilli powder
4 Tbsp tamarind pulp
salt to taste

Slit the chillies lengthwise and fry them for 1 minute in very hot oil. Remove and set aside. Slice the shallots, dry-roast the sesame seeds, peanuts, coriander seeds, coconut and half the cumin seeds, then allow to cool and grind to a smooth masala paste. Heat a further 3 tablespoons of oil in a pan, add the onion seeds, curry leaves, mustard and fenugreek seeds and remaining cumin seeds and when they start to crackle add the shallot. Sauté until the shallot is brown, then add the ginger and garlic pastes and sauté for a further 6 minutes. Next, add the turmeric and masala paste and cook for 4 minutes, stirring frequently. Pour in 150 ml (5 fl oz) of water and bring to the boil, then lower heat and simmer for 5 minutes. Add the green chillies, red chilli powder and tamarind and cook over a low heat for 10 minutes, then adjust seasonings to taste and transfer to a serving dish.

KOTMIR VONKAYA
(stuffed aubergines)

500 g (1¼ lbs) small round
aubergines
2 tomatoes
1 bunch coriander leaves
1 bunch mint leaves
2 large onions
8 green chillies
2 Tbsp ghee
oil for deep-frying
1 Tbsp cumin seeds
75 ml (3 fl oz) tomato juice

Slice the top off each aubergine and slit as if to quarter, but do not cut through to the base. Chop the tomatoes. Chop the coriander, mint, onions and chillies and grind together with a small quantity of water. Heat 1 tablespoon of ghee in a pan and add the cumin seeds. Stir until they start to crackle, then add to the ground vegetables. Mix well and drain off excess liquid so that the paste is smooth but not runny. Heat the oil and deep-fry the aubergines, then remove with a slotted spoon and drain off excess oil. Stuff the aubergines with three-quarters of the paste and set aside. Heat the remaining ghee and stir-fry the remaining paste for 2-3 minutes, then add the chopped tomato and tomato juice and continue to stir for a further 3 minutes. Finally, add the stuffed aubergines, adjust seasonings to taste and leave over a moderate heat until the aubergines are hot. Serve immediately.

Sour Aubergines and Fried Aubergines

BAGHARE BAINGAN
(sour aubergines)

600 g (1¼ lbs) small aubergines
75 g (3 oz) sesame seeds
75 g (3 oz) roasted peanuts
75 g (3 oz) grated dried coconut
100 ml (4 fl oz) oil
1 Tbsp cumin seeds
1 tsp mustard seeds
1 tsp onion seeds
0.5 tsp fenugreek seeds
8 curry leaves
1.5 Tbsp ginger paste
1 Tbsp garlic paste
1 Tbsp red chilli powder
1 tsp ground turmeric
125 g (4 oz) tamarind pulp
1 Tbsp ground coriander
salt to taste

Wash and trim the aubergines. Dry roast the sesame seeds, peanuts and coconut and grind to produce a masala paste. Heat half the oil in a pan and add the cumin, mustard, onion and fenugreek seeds together with the curry leaves. When the seeds start to crackle add the ginger and garlic pastes and sauté for 5-6 minutes, then add the chilli and turmeric. Next, add the masala and stir continuously until the oil rises to the surface. Add the tamarind and continue to cook until the oil oozes out of the pulp, then add 100 ml (4 fl oz) of water and bring to the boil. Lower heat and allow to simmer for 3-4 minutes, then sprinkle in the coriander and stir well. Meanwhile, heat the remaining oil in a fresh pan and fry the aubergines. Finally, add the aubergines to the sauce and allow to simmer for a final 2-3 minutes. Serve immediately.

KATHRIKAL VARUVAL
(fried aubergines)

4 large aubergines
75 ml (3 fl oz) fresh lemon juice
1 tsp ground turmeric
2 Tbsp ginger paste
1 Tbsp garlic paste
1.5 Tbsp red chilli powder
salt to taste
oil for deep-frying
lemon wedges

Quarter the aubergines, rinse in cold water and pat dry. Mix together the lemon juice, ginger paste, garlic paste, chilli powder and salt and rub over the aubergines. Set aside for one hour. Then, heat the oil in a pan and deep-fry the aubergines. Remove from the oil with a slotted spoon and drain off excess oil. Serve immediately garnished with lemon wedges.

PUDINE KI CHUTNEY
(mint chutney)

2 Tbsp chopped mint leaves
4 Tbsp freshly chopped coriander
2 tsp chopped garlic
1 Tbsp chopped green chillies
1 Tbsp chopped ginger
2 Tbsp chopped tomato
1.5 Tbsp pomegranate seeds
1 tsp chaat masala
0.5 tsp ground cumin
salt to taste

Place the mint, coriander, garlic, chillies, ginger, tomato and pomegranate seeds in a blender, add 100 ml (4 fl oz) of water and blend to a fine paste. Remove to a bowl and add the chaat masala, cumin and salt to taste. Mix thoroughly.

Note: If raw mangoes are available use in place of the tomato.

THAKKALI THOVIYAL
(tomato chutney)

1 kilo (2¼ lbs) tomatoes
4 cloves garlic
1.5 Tbsp oil
2 Tbsp mustard seeds
12 curry leaves
1 tsp red chilli powder
salt to taste

Chop the tomatoes and garlic and blend to a smooth paste. Heat the oil in a pan, add the mustard seeds and curry leaves and when they start to crackle add the tomato paste. Then, add the chilli powder and salt to taste and allow to simmer for 20 minutes, stirring frequently. Allow to cool and store in the refrigerator for 4-5 days.

SAUNTH
(sweet chutney)

200 g (7 oz) stoned dates
200 g (7 oz) tamarind
300 g (10 oz) palm sugar
2 tsp ground cumin
0.5 tsp ground fennel
0.5 tsp ground ginger
0.5 tsp red chilli powder
0.5 tsp black salt

Soak the dates and tamarind in 500 ml (18 fl oz) of water for 3 hours, then strain the liquid into a saucepan. Remove the date seeds and add the pulp to the pan. Add the palm sugar and bring to the boil. Stir until the sugar is dissolved, then remove the pan from the heat and add the remaining ingredients. Mix well and allow to cool, then transfer to a preserving jar and store in the refrigerator.

TIL KHOPRA
(coconut and sesame chutney)

3 large onions
10 green chillies
250 g (9 oz) grated coconut
100 g (4 oz) roasted sesame seeds
2 Tbsp freshly chopped coriander
75 g (3 oz) tamarind pulp
2 Tbsp fresh lemon juice
salt to taste

Chop the onions and chillies and grind together with the coconut, sesame seeds and coriander to produce a coarse paste. Add the tamarind, lemon juice and salt and stir to blend thoroughly.

RAITA
(spiced yoghurt)

2 tomatoes
250 ml (9 oz) natural yoghurt
4 Tbsp fresh milk (optional)
salt to taste
0.5 tsp red chilli powder
freshly chopped coriander

Chop the tomatoes into small dice. Whisk the yoghurt and if it is too thick use the fresh milk to make thinner. Add the tomato and season with salt to taste. Transfer to a serving bowl, sprinkle on the red chilli powder and garnish with a little freshly chopped coriander.

PALAKWALI DAHI
(spiced yoghurt with spinach)

800g (1¾ lbs) spinach
250 g (9 oz) natural yoghurt
salt to taste
6 cloves garlic
2 Tbsp oil
1 tsp cumin seeds
1 tsp mustard seeds
4 curry leaves
pinch red chilli powder
1 tsp freshly chopped coriander

Cook the spinach in boiling water, then drain thoroughly and chop. Whisk the yoghurt in a serving bowl, add the spinach and season with salt to taste. Chop the garlic. Heat the oil in a pan, add the cumin, mustard and curry leaves. When the seeds start to crackle add the garlic and sauté until golden, then add the chilli powder, stir and remove pan from the heat. When cool, add to the yoghurt, stir thoroughly and garnish with freshly chopped coriander.

MASALA BHAT
(spicy vegetable rice)

500 g (1¼ lbs) rice
2 large onions
6 green chillies
3 cloves garlic
1 small potato
1 small aubergine
100 g (4 oz) cauliflower
2 Tbsp oil
6 cardamom seeds
1 Tbsp cumin seeds
50 mm (2 inch) cinnamon stick
4 cloves
2 bay leaves
8 curry leaves
1 tsp ground turmeric
1 Tbsp red chilli powder
1 Tbsp ground coriander
75 g (3 oz) freshly grated coconut
75 g (3 oz) green peas
1 Tbsp palm sugar syrup
salt to taste
1 Tbsp fried chopped cashew nuts
1 Tbsp freshly chopped coriander

Soak the rice for 30 minutes, then wash under cold running water. Slice the onions, chop the chillies and garlic. Cut the potato and aubergine into small dice and the cauliflower into small florets. Heat the oil in a pan and add the cardamom, cumin, cinnamon, cloves, bay leaves and curry leaves. When the seeds start to crackle add the onion and sauté until it becomes golden, then add the green chilli, garlic, turmeric, chilli powder, coriander and prepared ground masala (see below) and stir-fry for 3-4 minutes. Next, add the coconut and continue to cook for 2 minutes, then add the peas, potato, aubergine and cauliflower together with 100 ml (4 fl oz) of water. Bring to the boil and retain over a moderate heat until the vegetables are half cooked, then add the syrup and rice and season to taste with salt. Add sufficient boiling water to cover the rice and cook over a moderate heat until the rice is tender.
To serve: transfer to a large dish, discard the cinnamon stick and garnish with cashew nuts and freshly chopped coriander.

To make the masala: grind together 1 tablespoon each of cumin seeds, coriander seeds and sesame seeds, 2 tablespoons of chopped peanuts, 2 tablespoons of grated coconut and 1 teaspoon of freshly chopped coriander.

PALAK PULAO
(mushroom rice)

250 g (9 oz) Basmati rice
250 g (9 oz) mushrooms
2 large onions
4 cloves garlic
25 mm (1 inch) knob fresh ginger
6 green chillies
100 g (4 oz) spinach leaves
4 Tbsp oil
1 Tbsp cumin seeds
6 green cardamom seeds
10 black peppercorns
4 cloves
salt to taste

Soak the rice in cold water for 15 minutes, then drain in a colander. Slice the mushrooms and onions, crush the garlic and chop the ginger, chillies and spinach. Heat the oil in a pan, add the cumin, cardamoms, peppercorns and cloves and when they start to crackle add the onion and ginger. Sauté until the onion browns then add the chilli and garlic and continue to sauté for a further 5 minutes. Next, add the mushroom and spinach and cook for 6 minutes, stirring frequently, then add the rice and salt to taste. Pour sufficient water into the pan to barely cover the rice and cook over a low heat until the rice is tender.

MUTTAR PULAO
(rice with peas)

500 g (1¼ lbs) Basmati rice
75 g (3 oz) ghee
5 green cardamoms
1 black cardamom
1 tsp cumin seeds
5 cloves
50 mm (2 inch) cinnamon stick
1 bay leaf
pinch of mace
1 tsp minced garlic
1 tsp finely grated ginger
150 g (5 oz) green peas
salt to taste

Soak the rice in cold water for 30 minutes, then drain in a colander. Heat the ghee in a pan and add the cardamoms, cumin, cloves, cinnamon, bay leaf and mace. When the seeds starts to crackle add the garlic and ginger and stir over a moderate heat for 1 minute, then add the peas and stir well. Next, add the rice and stir for 1 minute, then add salt to taste and pour in 1 litre of boiling water. Bring back to the boil and cook for 3-4 minutes, then reduce heat, cover and cook until the water has evaporated and the rice is tender. Discard the cinnamon stick, then transfer to a serving dish and let the steam escape before fluffing the rice with a fork.

Rice with Peas

TAMATAR PULAO
(tomato rice)

500 g (1¼ lbs) Basmati rice
1 onion
2 tomatoes
3 Tbsp ghee
1 tsp cumin seeds
6 cardamoms
6 cloves
1 tsp red chilli powder
2 Tbsp tomato paste
250 ml (9 fl oz) tomato juice
salt to taste
crispy fried onion rings

Soak the rice for 20 minutes, then drain thoroughly. Slice the onion and chop the tomatoes. Heat the ghee in a pan, add the cumin, cardamoms and cloves and when they start to crackle add the onion. Cook until the onion is golden, then add the tomato and chilli powder and cook until the tomato is soft, stirring frequently. Next, add the rice and stir-fry for 3 minutes, then add the tomato paste, juice and just sufficient water to cover the rice. Bring to the boil, then lower the heat, add salt to taste and cook until the rice is tender. Transfer to a serving dish and garnish with crispy fried onion rings.

Tomato Rice

PEETHI PURI
(deep-fried lentil bread)

75 g (3 oz) lentils
pinch of asafoetida
1 tsp red chilli powder
1 tsp ground coriander
400 g (14 oz) whole wheat flour
pinch of salt
ghee for deep-frying
flour for dusting

Soak the lentils for 30 minutes, then drain. Dissolve the asofoetida in 4 tablespoons of water and add to the lentils. Blend to a fine paste, then add the chilli powder and coriander, mix well and divide into 12 portions. Mix the flour, salt and approximately 250 ml (9 fl oz) of water, then knead to produce a medium-hard dough. Incorporate a little melted ghee and cover with a damp cloth. Set aside for 30 minutes, then divide into 12 portions and shape into balls. Dust with flour, re-cover and set aside for 10 minutes, then flatten each ball with a rolling pin into a flat disc. Next, place a portion of the prepared filling in the centre of each piece of dough and re-shape into balls. Cover once again and set aside for a further 10 minutes, then flatten into round discs, approximately 10 cm (4 inches) in diameter. To cook: heat the ghee in a large pan and deep-fry the puris until golden brown. Remove, drain off excess oil and serve immediately.

TAMATAR PURI
(tomato puri)

500 g (1¼ lbs) whole wheat flour
3 Tbsp tomato paste
1 Tbsp ghee
0.5 tsp salt
oil for deep-frying

Sieve the flour into a mixing bowl and make a well in the centre. Add the tomato paste, ghee and salt to the well. Knead for 3-4 minutes using just sufficient water to produce a semi-stiff dough. Roll out the dough and cut into 10 round puris. To cook: heat the oil until it is very hot and deep-fry the puris until they puff up and become golden brown. Serve immediately.

METHI THEPLA
(fenugreek bread)

2 bunches fenugreek leaves
500 g (1¼ lbs) wheat flour
150 g (5 oz) gram flour
300 g (10 oz) ground rice
1 Tbsp green chilli paste
1 Tbsp ginger paste
1 tsp salt
3 Tbsp natural yoghurt
3 Tbsp ghee

Wash the leaves and chop finely. In a bowl, mix the wheat flour, gram flour, ground rice, chilli paste, ginger paste and salt. Whisk the curd and add to the pan together with half the ghee. Mix thoroughly to produce a soft dough. Divide the mixture into small balls and flatten into round 'cakes'. Heat a griddle, moisten with the remaining ghee and fry the 'cakes' until golden on both sides.

LACHCHA PARATHA
(multi-layered bread)

450 g (1 lb) flour
0.5 tsp salt
2 eggs
100 ml (4 fl oz) milk
2 tsp sugar
0.5 tsp baking powder
pinch of bicarbonate of soda
2 Tbsp oil
150 g (5 oz) melted butter
flour for dusting

Sift the flour and salt into a mixing bowl. Beat the eggs. Warm the milk in a pan and dissolve the sugar, then add eggs, baking powder and bicarbonate of soda and set aside to ferment for 10 minutes. Add the mixture to the flour and mix thoroughly, then add approximately 175 ml (6 fl oz) of water and knead well. Gradually incorporate the oil, then knead again to produce a soft dough. Cover with a damp cloth and set aside for 30 minutes. Divide the dough into 6 portions and shape into balls, then flatten each with a rolling pin into a flat 'disc'. Place on a well-greased surface and stretch evenly on all sides until the 'discs' are very thin and approximately 35 cm (14 inches) in diameter. Brush the entire surface of each with melted butter and dust with flour, then gather together ensuring there are many folds. Roll again using a spiral movement to compress and set aside for 5 minutes, then flatten further to produce 'discs' approximately 17 cm (7 inches) in diameter. To cook: place on a heated griddle plate and half-bake, turning once, then pour the remaining butter all round and shallow-fry both sides until golden brown. Serve immediately.

MASALA KULCHA
(stuffed bread)

1 egg
1 Tbsp natural yogurt
2 Tbsp milk
1 tsp sugar
250 g (9 oz) plain flour
0.5 tsp baking powder
pinch of bicarbonate of soda
pinch of salt
1 Tbsp oil
2 Tbsp softened butter

Filling:
100 g (4 oz) cottage cheese
1 small onion
2 fresh green chillies
15 mm (3/4 inch) knob fresh ginger
1 Tbsp freshly chopped
coriander leaves

Beat the egg, add the yoghurt, milk and sugar and whisk. Sieve the flour, baking powder, bicarbonate of soda and salt into a mixing bowl and make a well in the centre. Add 100 ml (4 fl oz) cold water and knead well, then gradually add the egg mixture continually kneading to produce a soft dough. Cover the dough with a moist cloth, then add the oil and knead further. Punch the dough, then cover again and set aside for 90 minutes to allow to rise. Divide the mixture into four and shape into balls, then flatten in the palms of the hand. In the centre of each round place a portion of the prepared filling then seal and again shape into balls. Cover and set aside for 15 minutes. To cook: flatten each ball in the palms of the hands to produce rounds, approximately 12 cm (5 inches) in diameter. Place on a greased baking tray and cook in a pre-heated moderately hot oven for approximately 10 minutes. Remove, spread with butter and serve immediately.

To make the filling: grate the cottage cheese and chop the onion, chillies and ginger. Mix all the ingredients and divide into 4 portions.

Multi-layered Bread and Stuffed Bread

SHRIKHAND
(yoghurt pudding)

1 kilo (2¼ lbs) natural yoghurt
250 g (9 oz) sugar
large pinch of saffron
2 Tbsp milk
1.5 tsp ground cardamom
3 Tbsp chopped almonds
3 Tbsp chopped pistachios

Hang the yoghurt in a muslin cloth until all the liquid has drained off, then place in a bowl with the sugar and beat until smooth. Dissolve the saffron in the milk and add to the yoghurt together with the cardamom, almonds and pistachios. Stir to blend and transfer to individual dishes.

NARIAL KA MITHA
(coconut pudding)

4 eggs
100 g (4 oz) fresh breadcrumbs
1.25 litres (2¼ pints) milk
100 g (4 oz) granulated sugar
100 g (4 oz) grated coconut
2 Tbsp sultanas
2 Tbsp soft butter
1 Tbsp cardamom seeds
2 tsp grated lemon rind
3 Tbsp icing sugar

Separate the eggs and beat the yolks. Soak the breadcrumbs in the milk, then add the egg yolks, granulated sugar, coconut, sultanas, butter, cardamoms and lemon rind. Stir well and pour into a baking tray. Allow to stand for 15 minutes, then bake in a pre-heated slow oven until firm. Remove the tray from the oven and allow the pudding to cool. Next, beat the egg whites with the powdered sugar and spoon onto the pudding. Spread roughly over the surface and place in a very slow oven for 10-15 minutes, then serve immediately.

SHAI TUKRA
(bread pudding)

8 slices white bread
ghee for frying
500 g (1¼ lbs) sugar
pinch of saffron
2 litres (3½ pints) milk
0.5 tsp ground cardamom
2 Tbsp almond slivers
2 Tbsp chopped pistachio nuts
edible silver leaf for decoration

Remove crusts and quarter the bread slices diagonally. Heat the ghee and fry the bread until crispy. Dissolve the sugar in water and simmer until the syrup is thick, then add saffron. Let the syrup cool slightly then add the bread and leave it to soak for 5 minutes. Reduce the milk for 30 minutes, then cool and stir in the cardamom. To serve: arrange the bread slices on a large dish, cover with reduced milk and sprinkle almond slivers and pistachios on top. Finally, decorate with edible silver leaf.

SUZI KI PHIRNI
(semolina and nut pudding)

75 g (3 oz) semolina
75 g (3 oz) raisins
75 g (3 oz) cashew nuts
1.5 litres (2½ pints) full-fat milk
175 g (6 oz) sugar
0.5 tsp ground cardamom
2-3 drops rosewater
2 Tbsp pistachio slivers
saffron threads

Soak the semolina in cold water, then drain and set aside. Soak the raisins and blanch the cashewnuts in boiling water for 30 seconds. Boil the milk in a pan and retain over a moderate heat until reduced by half, then add the sugar and semolina. Stir continuously until the mixture reaches a custard consistency, then add the raisins and cashews and mix well. Remove the pan from the heat and continue to stir until the mixture reaches room temperature. Add the cardamom and rosewater and stir well, then transfer to individual serving dishes and chill. Just prior to serving garnish with pistachio slivers and saffron flakes.

GAJJAR HALWA
(carrot dessert)

600 g (1¼ lbs) carrots
750 ml (1¼ pints) fresh milk
150 g (5 oz) sugar
75 g (3 oz) ghee
pinch of ground cardamom
2 Tbsp sliced almonds
2 Tbsp sliced pistachios
1 Tbsp chopped cashewnuts
1 Tbsp raisins
edible silver leaf for decoration

Grate the carrots and place in a saucepan, together with the milk. Simmer over a moderate heat until the milk has evaporated, then add the sugar and stir until dissolved. Next, add the ghee and cook until the mixture turns a light golden colour, then add the cardamoms and cook slowly for a further 10 minutes, stirring frequently. Transfer to a serving bowl and sprinkle the nuts and raisins on top. Decorate with the silver leaf.

LAGAN NU CUSTARD
(egg custard)

3 litres (5¼ pints) milk
200 g (7 oz) sugar
6 egg yolks
3 egg whites
1 tsp rosewater
3 Tbsp ground almonds
pinch of nutmeg

Pour the milk in a saucepan and bring to the boil. Add the sugar and continue boiling until the sugar has dissolved and the milk has reduced by half. Then, remove pan from the heat and allow to cool. Beat the egg yolks and egg whites and add to the cooled milk, together with the rosewater, ground almonds and nutmeg. Blend well and pour into a greased baking dish and cook in a moderately hot oven for approximately 30 minutes. Serve hot or cold.

PALPAYASAM
(rice pudding)

300 g (10 oz) rice
1.5 litres (2¹/₂ pints) fresh milk
75 ml (3 fl oz) condensed milk
75 ml (3 oz) sugar
1 tsp ground cardamom
pinch of saffron
3 Tbsp almond slivers

Wash the rice and drain thoroughly. Bring the milk to the boil and add the rice, then reduce heat and allow to simmer for 10 minutes. Add the condensed milk and keep stirring until the liquid has reduced by half, then add the cardamom, saffron and almond slivers. Continue to stir until the mixture is very thick, then transfer to individual bowls. When cool, place in the refrigerator for 1 hour before serving.

KESARI KULFI
(pistachio ice-cream)

5 litres (8³/₄ pints) full fat milk
2 large pinches of saffron
300 g (10 oz) sugar
0.5 tsp ground cardamom
2 Tbsp blanched pistachio slivers
0.5 tsp rose syrup

Falooda:
300 g (10 oz) cornflour
0.5 tsp yellow food colouring

Use 2 tablespoons of milk to dissolve the saffron and pour the remainder into a large saucepan. Place the pan over a moderate heat and stir continuously until the milk has reduced by half, then add the sugar and stir to dissolve. Next, add the saffron, cardamom and pistachios and blend thoroughly. Remove from the heat and allow to cool, then pour the mixture into freezer trays and freeze for at least 6 hours, stirring occasionally. To serve: cut into slices, add the falooda and sprinkle the rose syrup on top.

To make the falooda: place a pan of water, approximately 1.25 litres (2¹/₄ pints), over a moderate heat and add the cornflour. Stir to dissolve, then add the colouring and continue to stir until the liquid has reduced to a jelly-like consistency. Then, force through a coarse sieve into a bowl of crushed ice.

GIL FIRDAVS
(pumpkin dessert)

125g (4 oz) rice
1 tsp butter
1¹/₂ litres (2¹/₂ pints) milk
125 g (4 oz) grated pumpkin
200 g (7 oz) sugar
75 g (3 oz) sultanas
3 Tbsp chopped pistachio nuts

Wash the rice and drain thoroughly. Melt the butter in a pan, add the rice and cook lightly over a slow heat, then grind to a powder. Boil the milk until it is reduced by half, then add the ground rice and the pumpkin. Stir until the pumpkin is almost cooked, then add the sugar and sultanas and continue to stir for a further 10 minutes. To serve: transfer to individual dessert cups and garnish with pistachios.

Pistachio Ice-cream

Glossary

In the editing of the original recipes some alterations have been made and most of the ingredients now listed should be generally familiar and readily available. The notes below are intended to give, in a very simple form, some useful information on Indian culinary terms, rather than act as a comprehensive glossary for this particular book.

AJWAIN
A small seed with an unusual, anise-like, flavour, regularly used in Indian cooking. Available in Indian grocery stores.

ANISEED
Strongly flavoured seeds frequently used in chutneys and sweet dishes.

ASAFOETIDA
An ingredient which adds a unique flavour and aids digestion. Has an unpleasant smell on its own and should be used extremely sparingly. Best to regard as 'optional'.

BOMBAY DUCK
Despite its name this is a very salty dried fish, usually sold in packets. It may be fried or grilled and served as a side dish with most curries.

CARDAMON
A seed pod of the ginger family often used whole in cooking, but the seeds alone are ground to produce the powdered form most commonly used in western kitchens. It is a very expensive spice but nevertheless an essential for the preparation of Indian food.

CHILLIES
Fresh chillies, both red and green, are used a great deal in Asian cooking and the quantities used (despite what any recipe may say) should always be a matter for personal taste. The real 'fire' comes from the seeds and for the more 'tender palates' these should always be discarded. Dried chillies are generally used whole but discarded before serving.

COCONUT MILK
Obtained by grating the flesh of a mature coconut and squeezing with water. On average the flesh of one coconut added to 150 ml (6 fl oz) of warm water and squeezed through a fine muslin cloth will produce a thick milk. To make a thinner milk the process should be repeated. Where 'thick' or 'thin' is not specified in a recipe use equal measures of both to make up the required quantity. The 'milky' liquid inside young green coconuts, referred to as **Coconut Water**, makes a refreshing drink but is seldom used for cooking.

CORIANDER
A fragrant ingredient used in curries and chutneys. The seeds may be used whole or ground to a powder. The leaves are generally chopped to either be used towards the end of the cooking process or as a garnish.

CUMIN
A small brown aromatic seed which is more often ground before use and is another essential ingredient in Indian recipes. The lesser-used **Black Cumin** has a darker seed and gives a stronger aroma.

CURRY LEAVES
These small aromatic leaves are best used fresh but if not available and the dried variety are substituted adjust quantities accordingly.

FENUGREEK
The leaves, fresh or dried and the seeds, dried and ground are basic ingredients in curries and are particularly good with seafoods. Because of the bitter taste should be used sparingly.

GARAM MASALA

A mixture of dry spices used in Indian curries and sold in jars at most major supermarkets. If making at home; place into a pan 3 tablespoons each of cloves, white and black cumin seeds, nutmeg and black peppercorns and 2 tablespoons of black cardamom and cinnamon bark. Place over a medium heat and dry-fry for 10-12 minutes, stirring frequently. Remove to a stone mortar and pound finely. Sift through a fine sieve before storing in an air-tight container.

GHEE

Pure butter fat with all the milk solids removed. It can be heated to much higher temperatures than butter and gives a very distinctive flavour. If not available, use clarified butter.

GINGER

A root stem with a very pungent flavour. It has a rough, thin skin which should be peeled off before using. Sliced, chopped or grated it adds a distinctive 'spice' to a dish. The commercially packaged powdered ginger has a quite different taste and is not a suitable substitute.

ONION SEEDS

Sold in Asian provision stores as **Kalongi**, these are frequently used in Indian kitchens but should be regarded as 'optional'.

PALM SUGAR

Often sold in Indian stores as **Jaggery**. This is a hard brown sugar made from the juice of the coconut palm flower. It's usually sold in solid cakes and crushed before use. Dark brown sugar, more readily available in the west, is an acceptable substitute.

SAFFRON

Used mostly in Northern Indian cuisine. This very expensive spice adds both fragrance and colour to desserts and special rice dishes.

TAMARIND

Pods of a tropical tree (originally African) which are treated to produce a sour-tasting pulp or liquid for use in curries. Dried and sold in packets.

Acknowledgement

In 1903 the Taj Mahal Hotel opened its doors in Bombay to instant acclaim and so laid the foundations for what was to become India's foremost hotel chain. Today, the Taj Group of Hotels offers accommodation in 35 destinations spanning India, ranging from luxury city properties to comfortable beach resorts and secluded country retreats (there is even a floating Palace on the tranquil Lake Pichola in the State of Udaipur). Outside India, the 'Taj Experience' can be enjoyed in 13 hotels in cities as widely dispersed as Colombo, London and Washington. London is also the location of the Bombay Brasserie which, since its opening in 1982, has proved to be one of the city's most consistently popular restaurants.

A paramount part of the Taj Group's policy has always been a wholehearted commitment to serving the finest cuisines, and the publishers are pleased to acknowledge the assistance given by the Group in the production of this book. Particular gratitude is due to Chefs Satish Arora and Arvind Saraswat, respectively Directors of Food Production at the Taj Mahal Hotel in Bombay and the Taj Palace Inter-Continental in New Delhi, who selected and coordinated recipes from hotels across India and who, with their staff, put in so much effort in preparing dishes for photography.

Index